SNAP SHOT™

Senior Editor Mary Ling
Art Editor Joanna Pocock
Editor Caroline Bingham
Designer Jane Thomas
Production Catherine Semark

A SNAPSHOT™ BOOK

SNAPSHOT™ is an imprint of Covent Garden Books.
95 Madison Avenue
New York, NY 10016

ISBN 1-56458-733-9

Color reproduction by Colourscan
Printed and bound in Belgium by Proost

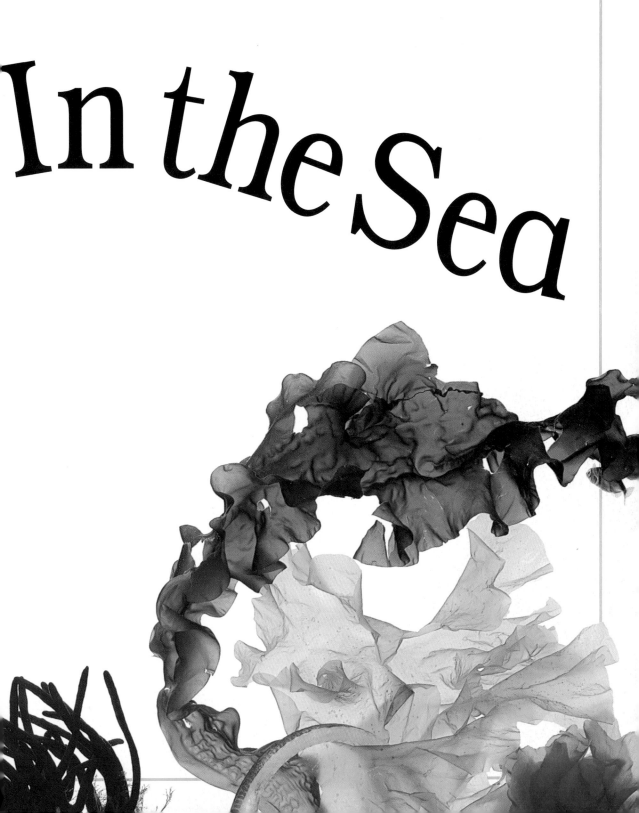

In the Sea

Contents

Sea lions

Can you swim like a fish?

Most of us can swim, and we can all enjoy water when we're in a boat. But unlike fish, if we want to explore the underwater world, we need tanks of special air to breathe.

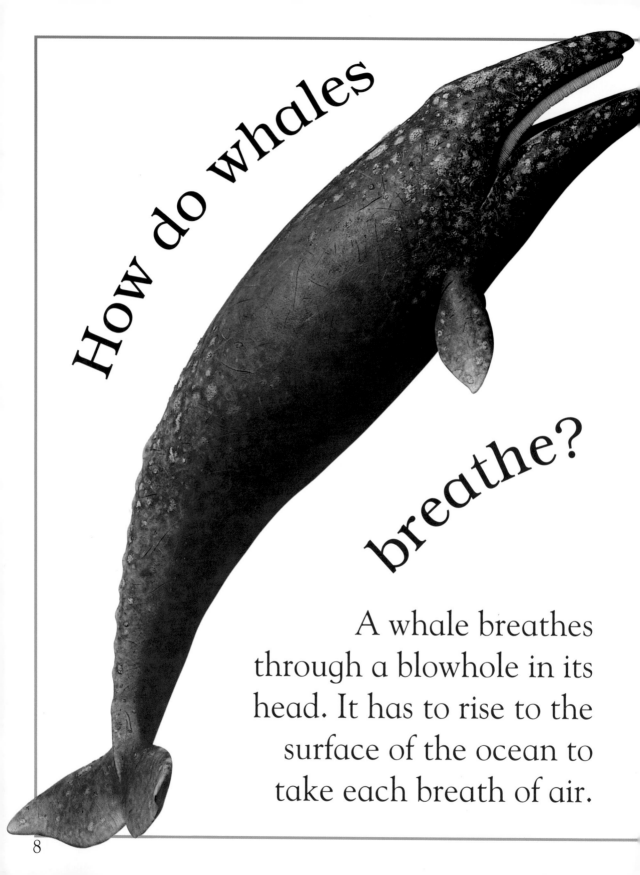

How do whales breathe?

A whale breathes through a blowhole in its head. It has to rise to the surface of the ocean to take each breath of air.

Let's go wake-surfing!

Dolphins love to play. Watch for them splashing and jumping in the wavy wake behind a boat.

A blanket of blubber

keeps out the cold.

Walruses have an extra-thick layer of fat, called blubber, under their skin. This keeps them warm in icy waters.

Color,

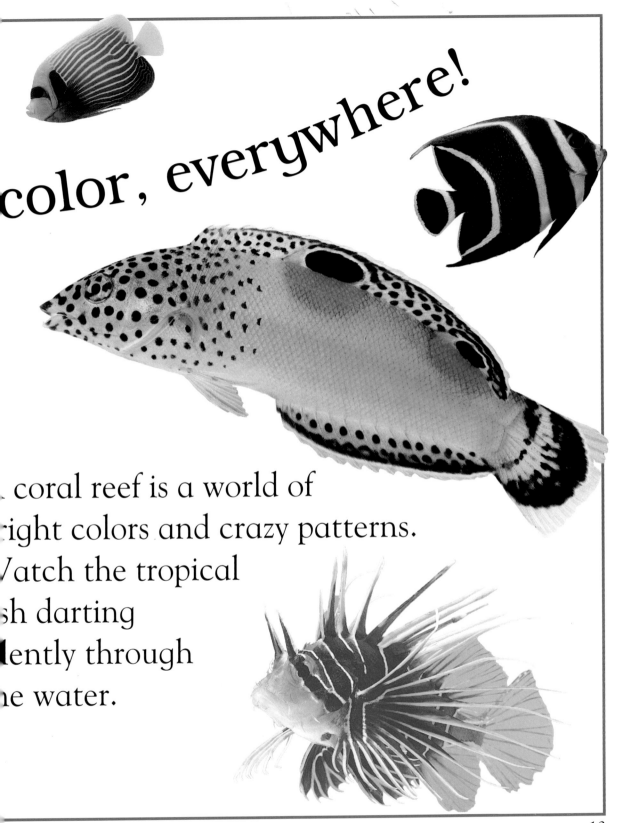

color, everywhere!

coral reef is a world of
right colors and crazy patterns.
Vatch the tropical
sh darting
lently through
ne water.

Sea horses use their curly tails to cling to coral when they want to stop for a rest.

Many sea creatures have unusual shapes. Just look at this sea urchin and sea cucumber!

strange creatures!

Where can you catch a star?

Look in a tide pool by the ocean and you will find all sorts of starfish and shells.

On the beach!

Pincer power!

Lobsters use their
huge pincers for
cutting and
crushing food.

How does a crab walk?

Sideways! This crab has six legs and a pair of pincers. It moves quickly, scuttling along the sandy seabed.

Seafood for supper?

Cormorants swoop down into the sea to catch fish in their hooked bills.

What noisy birds!

Sea gulls have a piercing cry as they hover overhead, looking for scraps.

Four fast swimmers!

These fish are all perfectly shaped for speeding through cool waters. Their silvery colors help them hide and hunt.

What do these boats do?

Tough little tugboats
pull and push great
big ships through
tricky waterways
and harbors.

Fishing trawlers pull huge nets behind them to catch fish.

Rescue me   at sea!

R.N.L.I. ROYAL SHIPWRIGHT

12-004

feboats rescue people
om stormy seas.
he rescuers wear life
ckets to help them
ay afloat if they fall
erboard. You
ould always wear
life jacket, too.

How does a sailboat move?

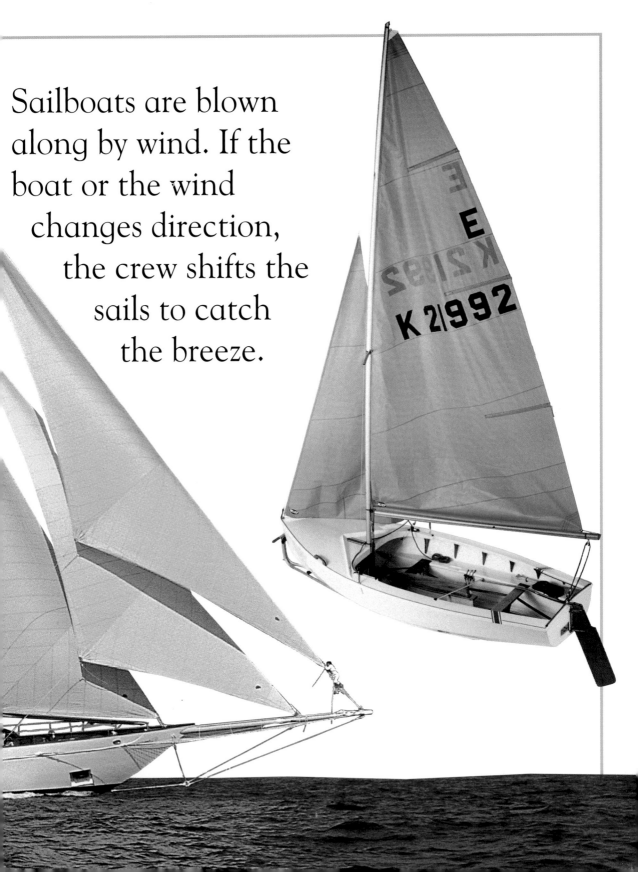

Sailboats are blown along by wind. If the boat or the wind changes direction, the crew shifts the sails to catch the breeze.

1. Spiny boxfish

Guess the

3. Angelfish

4. Starfish

2. Cowfish

sea shapes!

6. Stingray

5. Sea urchin

Answers on page 32

Answers

1. Square
2. Rectangle
3. Triangle
4. Star
5. Circle
6. Diamond